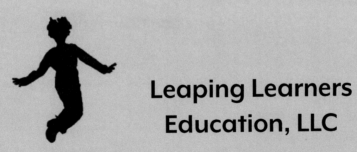

**Leaping Learners
Education, LLC**

For more information and resources visit us at:
www.leapinglearnersed.com

Photo Credits
Fish diver graphics © Alexey Bannykh/stock.adobe.com

Cover © Frolova_Elena/shutterstock.com; Title Pg. © Frolova_Elena/shutterstock.com; Pg. 2 © Studio 37/shutterstock.com; Pg. 4 © Dennis van de Water/shutterstock.com; Pg. 6 © GOLFX/ shutterstock.com; Pg. 8 © Andrea Izzotti/shutterstock.com; Pg. 10 © Rich Carey/shutterstock. com; Pg. 12 © Rattiya Thongdumhyu/shutterstock.com; Pg. 14 © Frolova_Elena/shutterstock. com; Pg. 16 © Kondratuk Aleksei/shutterstock.com; Pg. 18 © creativemarc/shutterstock.com; Pg. 20 © Rohrlach/stock.adobe.com; Pg. 22 © Stéphane Bidouze/stock.adobe.com; Pg. 23 © nikiteev_konstantin/shutterstock.com,

All designs by Sean Bulger
All other pictures by Sean Bulger or royalty-free from Pixabay.com

ISBN
978-1-948569-25-5

Dear Parents and Guardians,

Thank you for purchasing a *Fay Learns About* series book! After teaching students from kindergarten to second grade for more than seven years, I became frustrated by the lack of engaging books my students could read independently. To help my students engage with nonfiction topics, my wife and I decided to write nonfiction books for children. We hope to inspire young children to learn about the natural world.

Here at Leaping Learners, LLC, we have three main goals:

1. Spark young readers' curiosity about the natural world
2. Develop critical independent reading skills at an early age
3. Develop reading comprehension skills before and after reading

We hope your child enjoys learning with Fay. If you or your children are interested in a topic we have not written about yet, send us an email with your topic, and maybe your book will be next!

Thank you,

Sean Bulger, Ed.M

www.leapinglearnersed.com

Reading Suggestions:

Before reading this book, encourage your children to do a "picture walk," where they skim through the book and look at the pictures to help them think about what they already know about the topic. Thinking about what they already know helps children get excited about learning more facts and begin reading with some confidence.

Preview any new vocabulary words with your child. Key vocabulary words are found on the last few pages of the book. Have your children use each new phrase in their own words to see if they understand the definition.

After previewing the book, encourage your child to read the book independently more than once. After they have read it, ask them specific questions related to the information in the book. Encourage them to go back and reread the relevant section in the book to retrieve the answer in case they forgot the facts.

Finally, see if your child can complete the reading comprehension exercises at the end of the book to strengthen their understanding of the topic!

This book is best for ages 6-8
but. . .
Please be mindful that reading levels are a guide and vary depending on a child's skills and needs.

Fay Learns About...Seahorses

Written by Sean and Anicia Bulger

Table of Contents

Hi! My name is Fay. I love to discover and learn new things. In this book, we will learn about seahorses. Let's go!

Introduction

Do horses live underwater?

No! But seahorses do!

PG 2

Habitat

Where do seahorses live?

Seahorses live in **shallow**, grassy water. When the water is rough, seahorses move to deeper water to keep away from stormy oceans.

Body

What do seahorses look like?

Seahorses are fish. They have **gills** to breathe underwater. Unlike most fish though, seahorses do not have side fins. Instead they have a long tail for swimming.

PG 6

Seahorses can change their color to match their environment if they are in danger.

This makes it difficult for **predators** to find them.

Seahorses have great eyesight. Each eye can move in different directions. This helps seahorses find food.

PG 10

Diet

What do seahorses eat?

Seahorses eat small shrimp and **plankton**. They search for their food all over the ocean.

PG 12

Seahorses have a long neck and a mouth that points down. This helps them search small places for food.

PG 14

Predators

Which animals eat seahorses?

Seahorses do not have many natural predators because they are not very good to eat.

Crabs are one of the few animals that eat seahorses.

PG 16

Family

How do seahorses live together?

Seahorses stay with the same **mate** for life. Each morning, the pair meets and they do a special dance together.

PG 18

Seahorses are the only animals where the female gives the eggs to the male.

The male then carries the eggs in a pouch and finally gives birth to the babies.

Under Threat

Seahorses are under threat because people catch them to sell as pets, medicine, or gifts. When seahorses are taken from their environment, they suffer and die. We can help by not buying seahorses as pets, gifts, or medicine.

PG 22

The smallest seahorse is only 2 cm long!

PG 23

Seahorses have no teeth!

Glossary

A glossary tells the reader the meaning of important words.

Shallow – When there is only a short distance between top of water and the ocean floor

Gills – Organ that fish have for breathing underwater

Predator – An animal that eats other animals

Plankton – Small ocean animal

Mate – Partner

Draw a picture of a seahorse.

Choose 3 words from the glossary and write a sentence for each one.

1._____

_____

_____

2._____

_____

_____

3._____

_____

_____

Quiz

1. Where do seahorses live?
a. Oceans
b. Rivers
c. Lakes

2. Which word best describes a seahorses eyesight?
a. Poor
b. Great
c. Soft

3. What is the main idea of the section called "under threat"?
a. How seahorses can harm swimmers
b. Types of food seahorses eat
c. How seahorses are being threatened by people

Common core standards:
RI. 2. 1 - Questions 1, 2
RI. 2. 2 - Question 3

4. What do seahorses eat?

a. Fish

b. Plants

c. Plankton

5. True or false: Male seahorses give birth.

a. True

b. False

6. What does the picture on page 10 show you?

a. The eye of a seahorse

b. What seahorses eat

c. Where seahorses live

Common core standards:
RI. 2.1 - Questions 4, 5
RI. 2.7 - Question 6

Answer the following questions using information from the text:

1. Describe where seahorses live.

_____

_____

_____

_____

_____

2. Describe what a seahorse looks like.

_____

_____

_____

_____

_____

_____

3. Why don't seahorses have many predators?

_____

_____

_____

_____

_____

4. Why are seahorses under threat?

_____

_____

_____

_____

_____

Want to learn about rainforest animals? check out the "matt Learns About..." series!

Great for emerging readers ages 6-8

Want to learn about colors? Check out the "clayton Teaches you About..." series!

Great for early readers ages 4-6

Want to learn about Farm Animals? Check out the "Katie Teaches you About..." Series!

Great for early readers ages 4-6

Made in the USA
San Bernardino, CA
05 March 2019